A Look at
Impressionist
Art

Written by
J. Jean Robertson

Rourke
Educational Media
rourkeeducationalmedia.com

www.rourkeeducationalmedia.com

PHOTO CREDITS: Cover: © Burstein Collection; all but page 13: © Wikipaintings; page 13: © wime (inset)

Edited by Precious McKenzie

Cover and Interior design by Tara Raymo

Library of Congress PCN Data

A Look at Impressionist Art / J. Jean Robertson
 (Art and Music)
 ISBN 978-1-62169-876-0 (hard cover)
 ISBN 978-1-62169-771-8 (soft cover)
 ISBN 978-1-62169-976-7 (e-Book)
Library of Congress Control Number: 2013936785

Rourke Educational Media
Printed in the United States of America,
North Mankato, Minnesota

Also Available as:

Rourke
Educational Media

rourkeeducationalmedia.com

customerservice@rourkeeducationalmedia.com • PO Box 643328 Vero Beach, Florida 32964

Table of Contents

What is Impressionist Art?

This 1874 painting titled The Monet Family in their Garden *by Edouard Manet is of Claude Monet's family, a fellow impressionist painter.*

Impressionist art is the name for a style of painting that began in France in the 1860s and continued into the 1880s.

Art Fact

When pronouncing French names, the ending "s" and "t" are usually silent.

The Promenade, Woman with a Parasol
by Claude Monet, 1875

In Impressionist art, the painter uses lots of color. The painting gives an impression of the scene, with the imagination of the viewer supplying the details.

The Beginning

In 1874, Claude Monet displayed *Impression, Sunrise*, at a Paris art show. From that time on, all paintings in that style have been called Impressionist.

**Claude Monet
(1840–1926)**

Claude Monet was fascinated by light and the way changing light made things look different. He made groups of paintings that showed the same scene in different lights, such as sunrise, noon, and sunset.

Impressionist artists began painting scenes from the everyday lives of ordinary people. These paintings show the average French person in the late 1800s at work and at play.

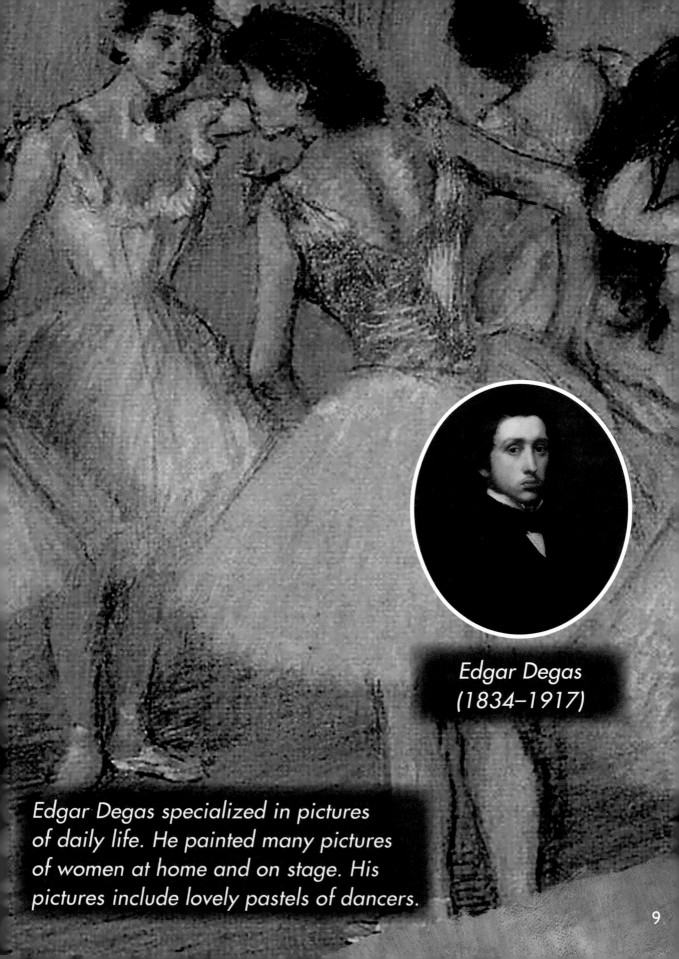

Edgar Degas (1834–1917)

Edgar Degas specialized in pictures of daily life. He painted many pictures of women at home and on stage. His pictures include lovely pastels of dancers.

For many years, most painting had been done in studios, but the Impressionist painters chose to paint outside. The play of natural light and shadow on the **subject** created different impressions from studio paintings.

Camille Pissarro's painting, The Boulevard Montmartre at Night *shows colors in limited light with the Impressionistic lack of detail.*

Camille Pissarro
(1830–1903)

Berthe Morisot was the leading French woman artist of the Impressionist period. Her paintings such as Reading with Green Umbrella (1873), showed the restrictions of her class and gender.

A new material saved time and mess. Can you guess what it was? It was paint that came in tubes. Before this invention, painters had to grind and mix their own **pigments** before they painted. The tubes of paint gave the artists more freedom to paint wherever they wished.

Berthe Morisot
(1841–1895)

The Masters

The Bridge at Argenteuil
Claude Monet, 1874

Because the Impressionist artists Alfred Sisley and Claude Monet lived near each other and worked together so often, they began to do things much the same way. This sometimes made it hard to tell who painted what picture.

L'Inondation à Port-Marly
Alfred Sisley, 1876

Alfred Sisley's landscape, L'Inondation à Port-Marly, *looks as though it could have been painted by Monet. Monet's* Bridge at Argenteuil *could be mistaken for a painting by Sisley.*

Georges Seurat was an artist-magician. His idea about painting was to paint, not with brush strokes, but with thousands of dots of paint. He expected the eye of the observer to fill in the gaps to create a whole image. This technique, called **pointillism**, had been tried before, but had never gained popularity.

Georges Seurat's 1884 painting, A Sunday Afternoon on the Island of La Grande Jatte, *is his most famous example of pointillistic painting.*

Paul Cezanne developed a different way of painting, which he called **internal perspective**. In his view, all of nature was a combination of cylinders, spheres, cubes, and cones.

Paul Cezanne's painting, Mont Sainte-Victoire, shows his idea of **geometric** shapes as the base of natural design, and also shows the use of color splotches typical in Impressionist painting. This painting was painted from 1885 to 1887.

Paul Cezanne
(1839–1906)

Pierre-Auguste Renoir
(1841–1919)

Pierre-Auguste Renoir's 1881 painting, Boating Party
Lunch, is his most famous work.

Pierre-Auguste Renoir was one of the three painters who formed the original Impressionist group. Renoir's work was easily recognized by its pretty, smiling girls wearing full dresses, hats, and carrying parasols. Although he was a master in Impressionist painting, Renoir moved away from Impressionism in his later paintings.

The Benefits of Art

The Starry Night
Vincent van Gogh, 1889

Many Impressionist paintings are available for us to study and enjoy. The **technique** of using splotches of color to give the feeling of dancing water and light is still used by artists today. The artists' willingness to try different ways of painting, even when others laughed, inspired others to try new ways of doing things.

Glossary

geometric (jee-uh-MET-rik): the outside surface of shapes, such as cubes and triangles

internal (in-TUR-nuhl): something that happens inside a person or thing

perspective (pur-SPEK-tiv): in art, distant things smaller than close ones, so they look further away

pigments (PIG-muhntz): the color from materials such as soils and plants, which can be used to make paints and dyes

pointillism (POIN-tuhl-iz-uhm): the theory or practice of creating a picture by using many small spots of color

subject (SUHB-jikt): in art, a person or thing that is being drawn, painted or sculpted

technique (tek-NEEK): a method or way of doing something that requires skill, as in the arts

Index

Websites

www.ArtSmarts4Kids:Impressionism

www.ducksters.com/history/art/impressionism.php

www.pragmaticmom.com/2013/01/impressionist-art-project-for-kids

About the Author

J. Jean Robertson, also known as Bushka to her grandchildren and many other kids, loves to read, travel, and write books for children. She, her husband, and children spent one summer traveling Europe and were privileged to enjoy much of the Impressionist art, which can still be seen today.

Meet The Author!
www.meetREMauthors.com

24